Military Vehicles

Jack Wesley

SCHOLASTIC INC.

New York   Toronto   London   Auckland
Sydney   Mexico City   New Delhi   Hong Kong

Read more! Do more!

After you read this book, download your free all-new digital activities.

You can show what a great reader you are!

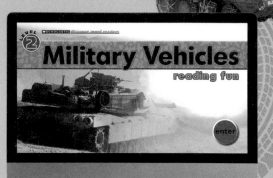

For Mac and PC

Look closer! Which vehicles are these? Click the button for the answers.

Take quizzes about the fun facts in this book!

Make a fighter jet
Zoom! Create your own superfast paper plane.

You will need . . .

Wheee!

Now click the numbers . . .

Do fun activities with simple step-by-step instructions!

Log on to

www.scholastic.com/discovermore/readers

Enter this special code: **L2MVNR6XCCP2**

Contents

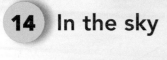

EDUCATIONAL BOARD:
Monique Datta, EdD, Asst. Professor, Rossier School of Education, USC;
Karyn Saxon, PhD, Elementary Curriculum Coordinator, Wayland, MA;
Francie Alexander, Chief Academic Officer, Scholastic Inc.

ISBN 978-0-545-67351-8

12 11 10 9 8 7 6 5 4 3 2 1   14 15 16 17 18 19/0

Printed in the U.S.A.   40
This edition first printing, September 2014

Scholastic is constantly working to lessen the environmental
impact of our manufacturing processes. To view our
industry-leading paper procurement policy,
visit www.scholastic.com/paperpolicy.

Land, air, and sea

Tanks roll across the land. Jets zoom through the skies. Battleships sail the seas. Military vehicles must be tough.

Ground force

Ground vehicles must protect the soldiers inside them. The Stryker has strong metal armor. It's quick. It takes soldiers to battle. Its machine guns fire back at the enemy.

Stryker

The eight wheels can speed along bumpy ground.

This lens helps the crew see at night.

Soldiers can get out the big door fast!

60 miles per hour

Crew: 2

The toughest ground vehicle is the tank. This 60-ton tank, the M1 Abrams, is nicknamed the Beast. It's heavier than six elephants! It has special tracks so that it can travel over rough ground. The soldier on the top fires a gun. This soldier is called the gunner.

M1 Abrams (the Beast)

Tanks through time

Mark 1
This was the first tank ever used in battle. It was used in World War I (1914–18).

T-34
This tank was used during World War II (1939–45). It had a powerful 76 mm gun.

M48
This was one of the US's main battle tanks in the Vietnam War (1954–75).

M1 Abrams
This is the US Army's main battle tank today.

45 miles per hour

Crew: 4

Boom! The enemy has blown up a bridge. How can tanks get across the river now? Bring in the Wolverine! This tank has its own bridge. It unfolds at the press of a button.

The bridge is ready in just five minutes. It can hold 70 tons—the weight of 35 cars!

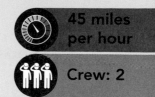
45 miles per hour

Crew: 2

The bridge unfolds to be 85 feet long.

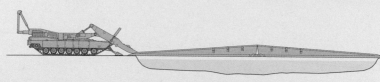

Wolverine Heavy Assault Bridge

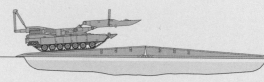

The smartest ground vehicle is a robot! BigDog has four legs and can follow commands. It carries food and weapons for soldiers.

BigDog can climb hills and cross rivers. It can travel through snow, sand, and mud. If it is knocked over, BigDog can even get back up on its own.

It's a fact!

BigDog

BigDog can find its own way.

Soldiers use real dogs, too. They can sniff out bombs.

4 miles per hour

Crew: none!

It never gets lost!

In the sky

The military has very special flying machines. Is the Osprey a plane or a helicopter? It is both! It takes off and hovers like a helicopter.

The Osprey can carry 24 soldiers to battle.

Then—*zoom!* In 12 seconds, it becomes a jet plane. It can fly at 288 miles per hour. It picks up and drops off soldiers quickly.

288 miles per hour

Crew: 3–4

Osprey

These soldiers are checking one of the rotors. Rotors make the Osprey hover.

NEW WORD

rotor
ROH-tur
A blade that turns to lift a helicopter is called a **rotor**.

SAY IT OUT LOUD

NEW WORD

troop

troop

A **troop** is a group
of soldiers.

SAY IT OUT LOUD

Chinooks

The Chinook is a
superstrong helicopter. It
has two 60-foot rotors. Rocky
mountainsides. Choppy seas.
Hot deserts. The Chinook
takes troops and supplies
anywhere, day or night.

The Chinook at work

The Chinook is used to deliver supplies. It can carry 11 tons.

There is space inside for 55 people, or 2 Land Rovers.

It is strong enough to lift a Jeep. It airlifts injured people.

Shhhh! These are spy planes. The enemy can't see or hear them. But they can see the enemy! They fly high above the ground. Special cameras take pictures of targets far below. Their bombs won't miss.

Stealth bomber

680 miles per hour

Crew: 2

The stealth bomber flies 9.5 miles above Earth.

Stealth bomber

The stealth bomber's longest single flight lasted 44 hours!

This is the fastest plane ever built.

Blackbird

The Blackbird flies 17 miles above Earth.

Blackbird

2,400 miles per hour

Crew: 2

You can't see me! The F-22 Raptor is invisible to the enemy. The enemy can't see it in the sky.

The Raptor is supersonic. It flies faster than the speed of sound!

F-22 Raptor

Famous fighters
The first fighter jets weren't as fast. But they won a lot of battles!

US, 1942

NEW WORD

supersonic

soo-pur-SAH-nik

A **supersonic** plane travels faster than the speed of sound.

SAY IT OUT LOUD

1,400 miles per hour

Crew: 1

UK, 1944

Germany, 1944

21

At sea

The navy has a big fleet of battleships. This 567-foot cruiser is one of the first to the front line! It is armed with missiles and guns. Helicopters take off from and land on the deck.

35 miles per hour

Crew: 400

USS *Princeton*

Dana Scott Canby is a lieutenant in the US Navy.

"I love going to sea on ships.... So it's really a dream come true.... You go to sea, drive the ship, manage the weapons systems, and get that sort of experience."

NEW WORD

fleet

fleet

A group of ships is known as a **fleet**.

SAY IT OUT LOUD

The battleship stands guard. A hovercraft takes troops and supplies back to shore. It rides the waves. It speeds through the surf.

The captain sits in the cockpit.

Air fills the skirt so that it floats.

A cushion of air keeps it afloat. It parks on land. The hovercraft is strong enough to carry a 60-ton tank!

50 miles per hour

Crew: 5

Landing Craft Air Cushion (LCAC) hovercraft

Fans at the back drive it forward.

A new US submarine is launched. Some of the crew stand on top and salute. With 12 missiles on board, it is ready for battle.

USS *North Carolina*

29 miles per hour

Crew: 143

Important decisions are made in the control room.

Submarines can travel 800 feet below the waves. They can stay there for several months at a time.

Crew members sleep on bunk beds. There are no windows in the bedrooms.

Divers can exit and enter through a hatch.

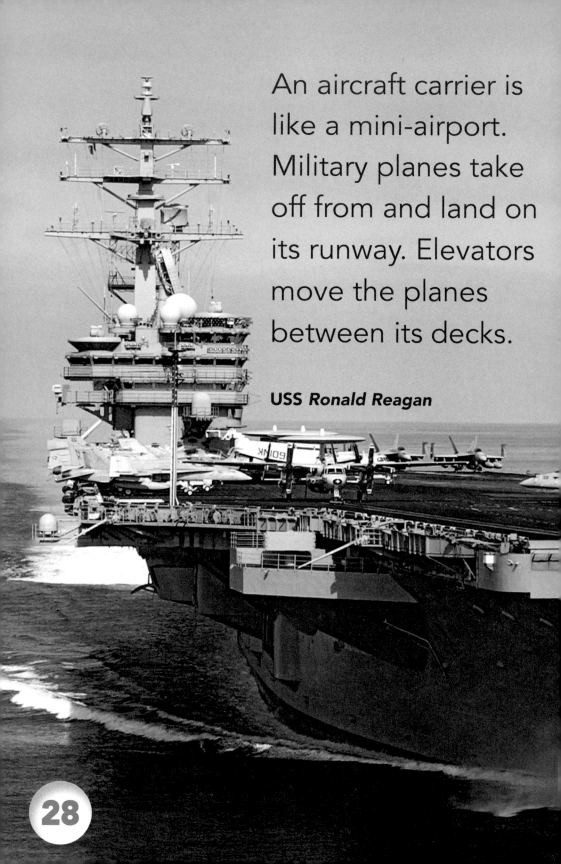

An aircraft carrier is like a mini-airport. Military planes take off from and land on its runway. Elevators move the planes between its decks.

USS *Ronald Reagan*

This carrier is 1,000 feet long. That's the length of three soccer fields! The military needs the best vehicles—often big, always powerful.

34.5 miles per hour

Crew: 6,400!

This aircraft carrier can hold 90 planes.

USS RONALD REAGAN
PEACE THROUGH STRENGTH
CVN 76

Glossary

aircraft carrier
A ship with a large, flat deck where planes and helicopters take off and land.

airlift
To move people or things by plane or helicopter.

army
The part of a country's military that fights on land.

battleship
A ship with many weapons that is used in war.

cockpit
The area in a boat or plane where the captain sits.

crew
A team of people who work together on a vehicle.

cruiser
A large, fast battleship.

fighter jet
A fast plane with guns and other weapons.

fleet
A group of ships.

front line
The place where two militaries meet and fight.

hatch
A small opening in a floor, deck, wall, or ceiling.

helicopter
A flying vehicle with large blades on top and no wings. Helicopters can hover and fly straight up and down.

hover
To stay in one place in the air.

hovercraft
A vehicle that moves across the surface of water on a cushion of air.

launch
To set a boat or ship afloat.

lieutenant
An officer in the military.

machine gun
An automatic gun that can fire bullets very quickly.

rotor
The blades that turn and lift a helicopter into the air.

submarine
A ship that travels underwater.

supersonic
Traveling at a speed faster than the speed of sound.

missile
A weapon that is aimed at a faraway target.

navy
The part of a country's military that fights at sea.

tank
A military vehicle covered in heavy armor.

troop
A group of soldiers.

Index

Images
Alamy Images: 5 tl (Air Collection), 3 bg (James Forte/National Geographic Image Collection), 1 (Mark Hamilton), 14 main, 15 main (Propaganda), 27 bl (RichardBakerScotland), 27 br (Ryan McGinnis), 19 t (Stocktrek Images, Inc.), 9 tl (The Art Archive), 17 t (Tony Hobbs), 18 t, 19 c (trekkerimages), 5 tr, 20 t, 21 t (US Air Force Photo), 16 main, 17 bg (US Army Photo), 29 t inset (US Navy Photo); CombatIndex.com/US Air Force/Airman 1st Class Russell Scalf: 14 inset; DARPA: 12 main, 13 main; Defense Imagery: 15 inset (Cpl. Kyle N. Runnels), 2 t (Gertrud Zach), 8 main, 9 b bg (Staff Sgt. Jacob N. Bailey), 7 tl (TSGT Mike Buytas, USAF); Defense Video Imagery and Distribution Center: 13 t photo (Cpl. Alfred V. Lopez), 10 explosion (Sgt. Ben Brody), 11 c (Staff Sgt. Jason Ragucci); Department of Defense: cover main (Gertrud Zach), 4 t, 6 bg, 7 bg; Dreamstime: inside cover top, 19 r silhouette (Aleksandr Mansurov), 17 br (Corsair262), 10 t bg (Elena Elisseeva), 18 t bg, 19 t bg (Eugenesergeev), inside cover center (Igor Kuzmin), 4 t bg, 5 t bg (Kanate), 10 b bg (Marek Uliasz), 24 bg sky, 25 bg sky (Matthew Collingwood), cover t bg (Robodread), inside cover bottom (Sergey Markov), 18 Earth, 19 Earth (Tomgriger); Getty Images: 2 bl (Barry Iverson/Time & Life Pictures), 32 (Stocktrek Images); iStockphoto: 9 Soviet flag (alfdaur), 23 paper (Electric_ Crayon), 6 tire tracks (Jamie Farrant), 8 tire tracks, 9 tire tracks (janraedschelders), speedometer throughout (Kristtaps), people icon throughout (Ieremy), 12 cartoon (memoangeles), 2 arrows (pagadesign), 9 American and British flags (pop_jop), 2 computers (skodonnell), tape throughout (spxChrome), 19 l silhouette (wagnerm25); National Archives and Records Administration/Department of Defense/Department of the Navy/US Marine Corps: 9 cl; Navy.mil: 26 main, 27 main (Chief Mass Communication Specialist Lucy M. Quinn), 24 t inset (Chief Photographer's Mate Johnny Bivera), 24 main, 25 main (Mass Communication Specialist 2nd Class Terah L. Mollise), 24 b inset, 25 inset; Royal Air Force: 21 bl; Shutterstock, Inc./ Paul J Martin: 3 fg; The Image Works/RIA Novosti/РИА Новости: 9 ctl; Tim Loughhead/Precision Illustration: 11 b; US Navy: 30, 31 (Gunnery Sgt. Steven Williams/NAVAIR), 6 inset (Journalist 2nd Class John J. Pistone), 26 b (Mass Communication Specialist 1st Class Jennifer A. Villalovos), 23 b inset (Mass Communication Specialist 3rd Class Kenneth Abbate), 22 main, 23 bg (Mass Communication Specialist 3rd Class Raul Moreno Jr.), 28, 29 bg (Photographers Mate 1st Class James Thierry); US Air Force: 20 b (National Museum of the), 17 bl (Senior Airman Mike Meares), 3 tr (Staff Sgt. Christopher Hubenthal), back cover t, 3 tl, 17 bc, 21 br; US Army: 23 t inset, 29 b inset (Institute of Heraldry), 7 tr, 9 cbl; US Marines: 4 b bg, 5 b (Cpl. Mark W. Stroud), 4 b (Lance Cpl. James Frazer), 10 tank (Sgt. Rachael K. A. Moore), 5 c (Staff Sgt. Matt Epright).